Juliana Mendonça

Planting a Seed Inside Myself

Illustrations by Marlowa Pompermayer Marin

To Isabella!

Your outlook on life fills my heart with joy.

Gratitude!

I would like to express my sincere gratitude to my family and dear friends who collaborated with me in so many ways, especially, my husband for his constant encouragement, Vera Amaral, Silvia Salles, and Scott Horton for their review and suggestions, Marlowa for the inspiring artwork, and González Pecotche for his generosity and life example.

Juliana Mendonça

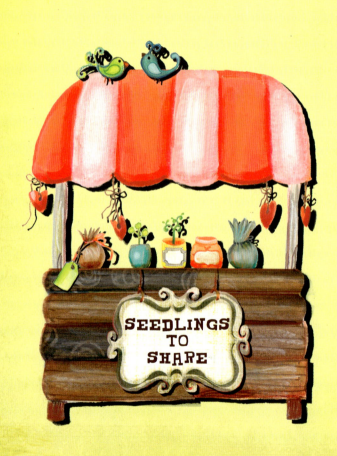

Juliana Mendonça

Planting a Seed Inside Myself

Illustrations by Marlowa Pompermayer Marin

Text Copyright © 2013 by Juliana Mendonça.
Cover and internal illustrations copyright © 2013 by Marlowa Pompermayer Marin.
Cover and internal design © 2013 by Marlowa Pompermayer Marin

All rights reserved. Published in the United States by Planting a Seed Books, Round Rock, TX.
Printed in China
July, 2013
Printed by Everbest Printing (Guangzhou, China), Co. Ltd
111005

Publisher's Cataloguing-in-Publication data

Mendonça, Juliana.
    Planting a Seed Inside Myself / by Juliana Mendonça ; illustrated by Marlowa Pompermayer Marin. – 1st. edition – Round Rock, TX : Planting a Seed Books, 2013
    p. cm.
    ISBN-10: 0989004902
    ISBN-13: 978-0-9890049-0-9
1. Children -- Conduct of life -- Juvenile literature. 2. Children -- Conduct of life. I. Title.

179.9 -- dcc22
Library of Congress Control Number: 2013904872

Planting a Seed Books

PLANTING a SEED INSIDE MYSELF

Dear Parents and Teachers:

This book was inspired by the Logosophical Pedagogy, a learning process created by Carlos Bernardo González Pecotche, the Argentine humanist, educator, and thinker.

For more than 50 years, the Logosophical Pedagogy has been applied with successful results in K-12 schools in Argentina, Uruguay and Brazil. In addition to working with subjects that are part of a standardized curriculum in these schools, prepared teachers also guide children through a process of discovering their own inner reality and the role that thoughts and feelings play in their choices and thus in the outcome of their experiences. This work awakens the intent in children to become better human beings and to assume an active role in their own lives and in their communities.

My goal with this book is to share an analogy with you and your children for two of the main concepts presented by the Logosophical Pedagogy: the concept of *thoughts* and the concept of *feelings*.

From a very early age, children are capable of assuming an active role in identifying, classifying, and selecting their own thoughts, as well as cultivating useful thoughts and feelings that will ultimately help them become happy and self-confident human beings.

This learning process end up becoming the work of a lifetime, and we, as adults, can also immensely benefit from it. So, let's all learn to plant seeds inside ourselves!

There is a field inside of us that deserves the best seeds we can find.It is a very special place where anything that we plant and care for is able to grow and thrive.

That's why we need to be careful when choosing the plants we grow in this field, because even if they seem good choices at first, they can easily turn out to be useless, or worse!

And don't ignore the weeds that can grow in this field, because they not only take away space and energy from the good young plants that we are trying to grow, but they are also hard to get rid of.

Where do these seeds come from?
We are born with some of these seeds. If we give them proper light and good soil, they will sprout and start to grow. But if not, they will just lie there, asleep, waiting for the right nutrients that will wake them up at a later time.
Other seeds come from all around us. They can come from parents, teachers, friends, or even the TV shows and movies that we watch, the books we read, the people we meet, the places we go, and so on.
When we take a seed inside of us, it may instantly start to grow.
But that doesn't mean it will turn out to be a useful plant.
It's important to observe and to know.

What should we observe?

It is important to start observing the effects that each one of these little plants has in our daily life, because they can make us feel or act in different ways. We should ask ourselves: Do I like feeling this way? Do I like acting this way? Do my friends and family enjoy my company when I act this way?

Take for example the beautiful plant called generosity.

This precious plant makes us feel so happy when we are able to make others happy around us. Don't we all feel happy when we have the opportunity to share a book or a toy with a friend? Or to take turns when we play? Try to remember a day when it felt really good to share something with a friend. That's the work of generosity. But, if we let the weed called selfishness take the place of generosity, then it usually causes lots of trouble. We might end up having to play by ourselves or sit alone in our room, wasting the opportunity to share good times with our friends. When this happens, we probably won't feel very good about it, and we might even imagine that nobody cares about us. But this is not true. The problem is allowing the weed called selfishness to take up space inside of us.

Another example is one very useful plant we call order. It is so good to know exactly where our objects are when we need them. This way, we don't waste our time looking for them, and we can carry on with our activities without interruption. On the other hand, if disorder is the plant growing inside of us, it will try to make us believe that leaving our toys, clothes, and other belongings spread all over the place causes no harm at all.

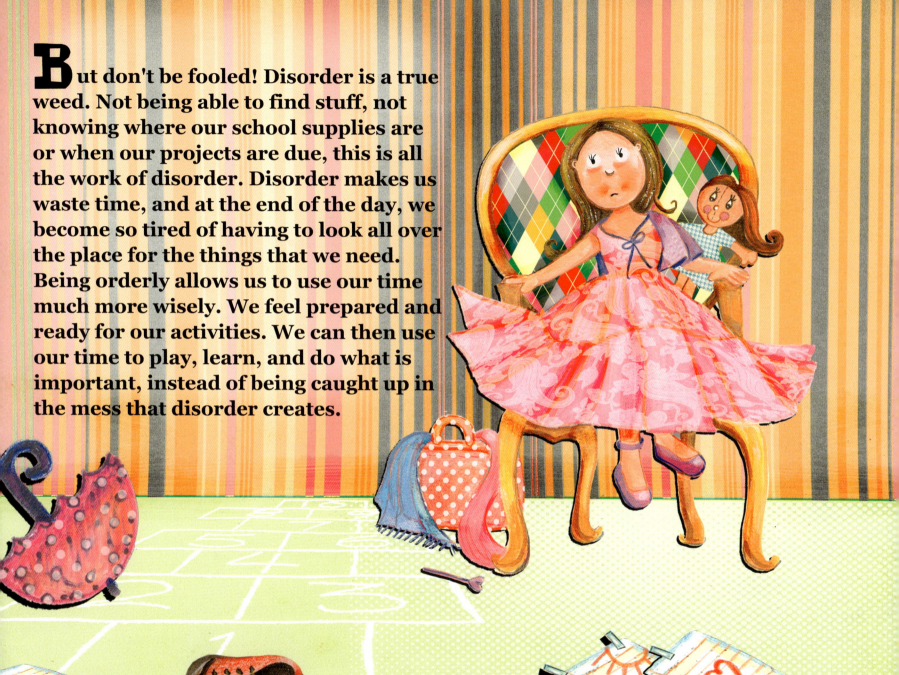

But don't be fooled! Disorder is a true weed. Not being able to find stuff, not knowing where our school supplies are or when our projects are due, this is all the work of disorder. Disorder makes us waste time, and at the end of the day, we become so tired of having to look all over the place for the things that we need. Being orderly allows us to use our time much more wisely. We feel prepared and ready for our activities. We can then use our time to play, learn, and do what is important, instead of being caught up in the mess that disorder creates.

From these examples you can see why it is so very important to carefully select the plants that we allow to grow in our inner fields. Observation is the key to discovering which plants are the really good ones and which are the weeds. By observing our inner field and the effects that each plant has in our daily life, we will definitely start learning how to select the plants that make us feel, and act, just right.

So, would you like to try an exercise?
Let's take a look inside of ourselves and try to find
this special field. It might be difficult at first, but
the more we try, the more we'll start to see it.
For example, when we lend a helping hand to our
parents, to our friends, or to our teacher at school,
how does that make us feel? Don't we feel good
about it? Being a good helper and willing to help
out when it's needed is such a noble trait.
We could say that this willingness to help out is the
result of a little plant we carry inside called
collaboration. There is no doubt this is a very
good plant to keep around, and we should
give it lots of nutrients so that it can grow
strong and strong every day.
So the next time help is needed
around you, try to remember how it felt
the last time you lent a helping hand,
because just by remembering it, you'll
want to feel that way again. Putting the plant
known as collaboration into practice will act as a
great fertilizer, helping it grow a long way.

We may also find a little plant inside of us that makes us very happy learners. This plant gives us energy and encourages us to learn as much as we can at school and anywhere we go. That's another plant that deserves our very best care. Isn't it so exciting to learn something new every day and discover that there are always new things to learn?

Now, we will probably find a few weeds in our fields, too. Sometimes we might not treat our friends or family members the right way. We might say hurtful words or make them sad. How do we fell when the people we care about are sad?

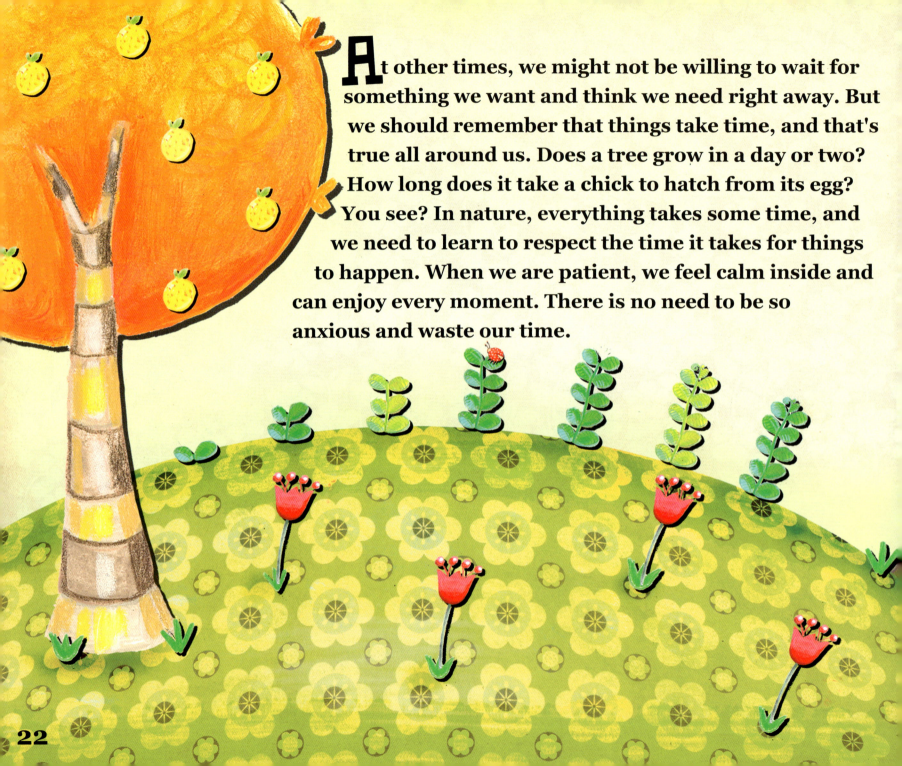

At other times, we might not be willing to wait for something we want and think we need right away. But we should remember that things take time, and that's true all around us. Does a tree grow in a day or two? How long does it take a chick to hatch from its egg? You see? In nature, everything takes some time, and we need to learn to respect the time it takes for things to happen. When we are patient, we feel calm inside and can enjoy every moment. There is no need to be so anxious and waste our time.

Caring for this little plant called patience is very important. It will grow stronger and stronger each and every day as we try to get rid of the weed called impatience that keeps getting in its way. But there is also a secret to patience, did you know? We don't need to sit still while we wait. Instead, we can do other things that make the waiting fun. Try it and let me know how you've done.

There are so many plants worth growing in this inner field that it's hard to even name them all. The secret to choosing the best plants is to observe how we feel and how others feel around us. There is always time to change our ways and to replace a weed with a great plant.

Learning to look inside of our own special field is one of the secrets to happiness. The more we learn to cultivate the good plants and to get rid of those pesky weeds that just get in the way, the better gardeners we'll become each and every day.

And if we keep practicing these special gardening tips, we will even be able to select our own special seeds. These seeds will come from deep down inside of us, and they will represent what we want out of our own lives. If we want to become a better person, or to grow and learn more each and every day, then we will definitely select beautiful seeds that will make this internal garden our favorite place to stay.

And when you have great plants growing inside, you will want to do what all good gardeners often do, and that is share your seeds with others so they can grow great plants, too. You'll do this by being a great role model and by teaching others that they, too, can start cultivating their inner field as you are now learning how to do.

Well, that's about it for now. We'll talk again some other time when I'll tell you about each kind of plant and how to strengthen or weaken it according to its intent.

But before I go, let me end by sharing with you the names of just a few of my favorite plants:

Patience, collaboration, love, perseverance, gratitude, generosity, discipline, order, friendship, responsibility, tolerance.

GLOSSARY

Anxious: Nervous or worried.

Collaboration: The act of working together with a purpose.

Effects: Consequences, something that happens because of an action or fact.

Instantly: Immediately.

Intent: Purpose, goal, intention.

Interruption: To cause something to stop.

Noble: Excellent, admirable.

Nutrients: Substances that provide nourishment for growth and development.

Proper: Correct, adequate.

Thrive: To grow or develop well.

Trait: Quality or characteristic.

Useless: Something that does not have a positive purpose or an actual purpose on a certain situation.

Wisely: With good judgment and intelligence.

My name is Juliana Mendonça, and this is my first children's book. I have always loved to learn. I have a Bachelor's degree in Electrical Engineering, a Master's degree in Information Studies from UT Austin, and I currently work as a technical translator. I have many other interests and hobbies, but one of my favorite activities is to study about my inner field, getting to know the plants I have inside, choosing and strengthening the best ones, and getting rid of the weeds. This is not an easy task, but it's worth every effort. I would love to hear your impressions about this book. If you would like to share your thoughts with me, write me a note at: juliana@plantingaseedbooks.com

Marlowa Pompermayer Marin is originally from Brazil. She has a degree in Visual Arts and was able to accomplish her life-long dream of becoming an illustrator. By illustrating Planting a Seed Inside Myself, Marlowa has a new opportunity to bring her drawings and paintings to the far away fields of the English speaking countries. "It's a great joy to illustrate stories inspired by the Logosophical Pedagogy, an educational method whose study has been offering me valuable cognitions." Marlowa lives and works in Chapecó, Brazil with her husband and two children. Check out her beautiful and inspiring art work at www.marlowa.com.br